Do Great Things for God

Joni Eareckson Tada

The Girl Who Learned to Follow God in a Wheelchair

Kristyn Getty

Illustrated by Hsulynn Pang

Joni was born the youngest of four sisters in Baltimore, USA. She was called Joni after her dad, John. He had been hoping for a boy!

Joni had sparkling blue eyes, a clever mind, and lots of energy. She loved to ride horses... to play lacrosse... and to go on adventures.

Joni grew up going to church and singing hymns with her family. But even though she knew about Jesus, she did not know him as her friend.

When she was 15, Joni went to a church camp. There, she understood Jesus Christ's great love and forgiveness and how much she needed him.

She prayed to God, "Instead of doing things my way, I want to follow Christ's way." She wondered where his way would take her.

When Joni was 17, one day she went swimming in a bay with her sister. She loved swimming! She dived off a float, into the water. But the water was too shallow for diving. Joni's head hit the bottom – and suddenly she could not move.

Her sister saw Joni floating in the water.

She pulled her out and called to someone to phone for an ambulance.

In the hospital, Joni and her family heard some very bad news. Joni's neck was broken. Her hands would never work properly again, and her legs would never work at all. She would have to stay in the hospital for a long time.

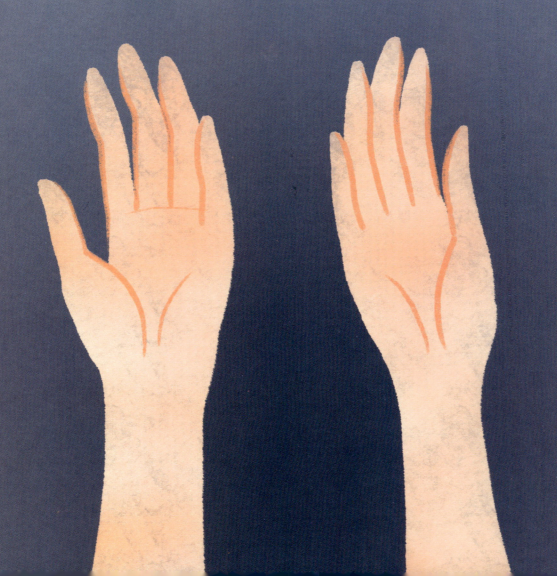

In a moment, all her life had changed. She felt afraid and had many questions. What would she do now? Who would take care of her?

Joni had to work out how to manage.
Little by little, she learned...

how to move her
shoulders and arms...

how to sit up in
a wheelchair...

how to scoop up her food
with a special spoon that was
attached to her hand with
leather straps...

and how to rely on helpers
through the day and in the night.

Joni's friends and family visited her often.

One day, a friend even sneaked a little puppy into the hospital. She loved feeling its soft fur on her face!

In the hospital, Joni had a lot of time on her own. Sometimes, she felt very sad. Sometimes, she felt very angry. Why had God let this happen? Did God care about her? Why didn't he fix her legs?

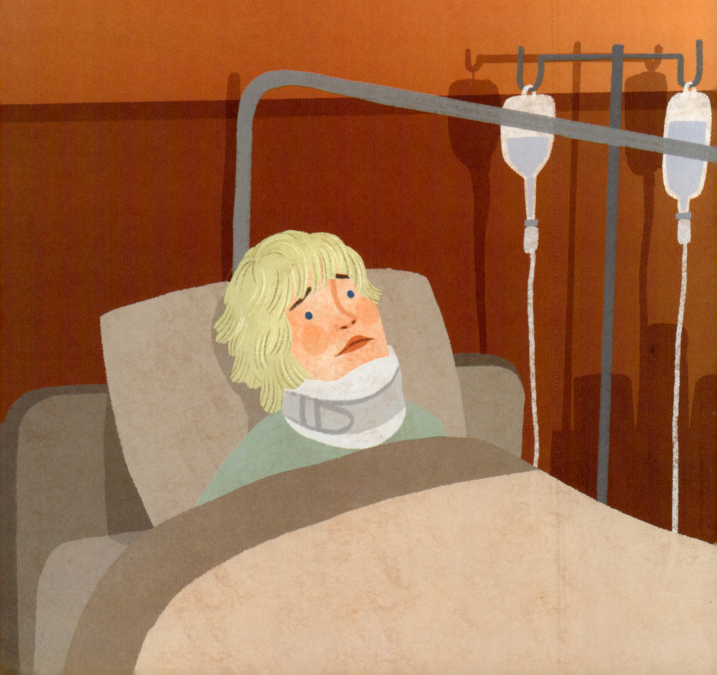

It was easy to trust God when she was healthy and happy. But did she want to follow God now that life was so hard?

Both while she was in the hospital and when she was able to go home, Joni read her Bible. It showed her that God was not surprised by her accident. It reminded her that God promised to care for her and help her, even if he didn't make her better.

Joni read that "in all things God works for the good of those who love him" (Romans 8:28). She realized that God loved her and that he could use even her accident for good.

"Lord, show me how to follow you in this wheelchair," Joni prayed.

Joni became a friend to those who had disabilities like her. She told them how much God loved them.

She began to paint beautiful pictures by holding a paintbrush in her mouth.

She met a lovely man called Ken Tada, and they got married.

She started "Joni and Friends," which sends wheelchairs to people all over the world who can't afford to buy one.

She hosts camps to take care of families with disabilities.

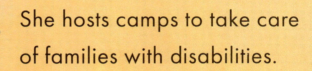

She gives good ideas to governments and churches to help people with disabilities.

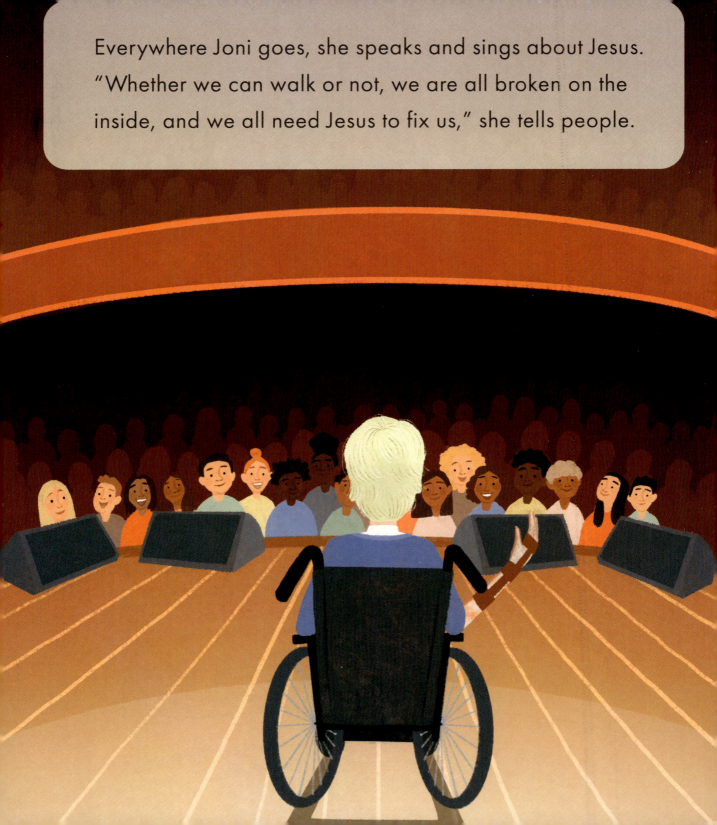

Joni has been in a wheelchair for over fifty years.

Every day she has pain in her body and a great longing in her heart for a new one.

But her blue eyes still sparkle because she can sing, "My hope is built on nothing less than Jesus' blood and righteousness." When Joni sings about God, she remembers that he is big and strong and wise enough to trust.

One thing Joni loves is spending time with children. She enjoys answering their questions and talking to them about Jesus.

Once, a young child asked her,
"Joni, will you ever walk again?"

"Yes," said Joni. "One day, I will be in heaven, and Jesus will give me new legs. And when I get my new legs, the first thing I'll do is kneel down to worship him."

Until then, Joni knows God has work for her to do, especially showing friendship to those with disabilities.

Do you know people whose bodies don't work as well as they'd like? Joni would love it if you were a friend to them. But what she would love most is for you to know her greatest friend as your friend too – the Lord Jesus.

And I know that because... she told us!

A Prayer You Could Pray

If you would like Jesus to be your friend, here is a prayer you can say:

Dear Lord Jesus,

Thank you for dying on the cross to take away all my sin – all the ways that I have not loved and obeyed you as my King.

Please forgive me and give me new life. May I trust in you as my Lord and Savior and greatest friend, in good times and especially in bad times.

Teach me how to follow you until I see you in heaven. Amen.

Questions to Think About

1. Which part of Joni's story did you like best?

2. Joni trusts that "in all things God works for the good of those who love him" (Romans 8:28). Do you love Jesus? Why is it good to know that he is always working to help and care for everyone who loves him?

3. Joni loves it when people are a friend to others whose bodies don't work as well as they'd like them to. Do you know anyone like that? How can you be a good friend to them?

4. What ideas does Joni's story give you about how you might serve Jesus when you are older?

5. What one truth about God would you like to remember from this story?

Joni Eareckson Tada

- **October 15, 1949** – Joni is born in Baltimore, Maryland. Her parents are John and Lindy, and she has three older sisters.

- **July 30, 1967** – Joni dives into shallow water in Chesapeake Bay and is paralyzed. She spends the next two years in the hospital.

- **1969** – Joni leaves the hospital.

- **1972** – A family friend puts on an exhibition of Joni's artwork, all drawn with a paintbrush held in her mouth. Lots of people buy her paintings for a total of over $1,000 (over $7,000 in today's money). Instead of writing her name, Joni signs all her paintings "P.T.L.," which stands for "Praise the Lord."

- **1976** – Joni publishes her autobiography, *Joni: The Unforgettable Story of a Young Woman's Struggle against Quadriplegia and Depression*. It has now been translated into more than 38 languages, and there are 5 million copies in print. (Joni has now written over 50 books. At first she wrote by holding a pen in her mouth; today, she uses a computer program that turns her voice into written words.)

- **1979** – Joni and Friends (JAF) is founded.

- **1980** – *Joni* is released as a film.

July 3, 1982 – Joni marries Ken Tada.

1982 – The Joni and Friends Radio program begins. It teaches the Bible, encourages listeners, and helps people be more aware of what it's like to live with a disability.

1988 – US President Ronald Reagan asks Joni to be part of the National Council on Disability, helping the government care for people with disabilities.

1994 – Wheels for the World begins. Its aim is to send wheelchairs to parts of the world where many people can't afford to buy one and to tell those people about Jesus.

2007 – The JAF International Disability Center opens in Agoura Hills, California.

2012 – Joni becomes a member of the National Religious Broadcasters Hall of Fame.

2014 – Wheels for the World delivers the 100,000th donated wheelchair.

2017 – Joni sings "Hallelujah! What a Savior!" at the first Sing! Conference, organized by Kristyn and her husband Keith.

2019 – Joni and Friends celebrates its 40th birthday.

Interact with Joni's Story!

Download Free Resources at
thegoodbook.com/kids-resources

Joni Eareckson Tada

Born 1949

"In all things God works for the good of those who love him."

Romans 8:28

"Joni's story is amazing, and Kristyn tells it beautifully, without shying away from the painful parts. But even more amazing is the way Joni's story so joyfully points us to Jesus."

ANDREW PETERSON, Singer; Songwriter; Author, *The Wingfeather Saga*

"Joni Eareckson Tada shows us by her example that the path to our destiny, or the path of a loved one to theirs, may lead through suffering. In this simple children's book, Kristyn Getty has underscored faith in and friendship with Jesus as essential if we want to come through the worst of times with blessings for ourselves — and for others."

ANNE GRAHAM LOTZ, Bible Teacher; Author, *Just Give Me Jesus*

Joni Eareckson Tada
© Kristyn Getty 2024
Illustrated by Hsulynn Pang | Design and Art Direction by André Parker
Series Concept by Laura Caputo-Wickham
"The Good Book For Children" is an imprint of The Good Book Company Ltd.
thegoodbook.com | thegoodbook.co.uk | thegoodbook.com.au
thegoodbook.co.nz | thegoodbook.co.in
ISBN: 9781802540673 | JOB-007696 | Printed in India